GUIDE TO THE EXHIBIT

GUIDE
to the
EXHIBIT

Lisa Allen Ortiz

perugia
PRESS

FLORENCE, MASSACHUSETTS
2016

Perugia Press extends deeply felt thanks to the many individuals whose generosity made the publication of *Guide to the Exhibit* possible. Perugia Press is a tax-exempt, nonprofit 501(c)(3) corporation publishing first and second books of poetry by women. To make a tax-deductible donation, please contact us directly or visit our website.

Book design by Susan Kan, Jeff Potter, and Lisa Allen Ortiz.

Cover art is "Cystorseira fibrosa," from *Photographs of British Algae: Cyanotype Impressions*, by Anna Atkins (1799–1871), from the Spencer Collection at The New York Public Library, http://digitalcollections.nypl.org/collections.

Author photograph by Chloe Ortiz. See chloeortizphotography.com.

Library of Congress Cataloging-in-Publication Data

Names: Ortiz, Lisa Allen, author.
Title: Guide to the exhibit / Lisa Allen Ortiz.
Description: Florence, Massachusetts : Perugia Press, 2016.
Identifiers: LCCN 2016013509 | ISBN 9780979458293
Classification: LCC PS3615.R822 A6 2016 | DDC 811/.6--dc23
LC record available at https://lccn.loc.gov/2016013509

Perugia Press
PO Box 60364
Florence, MA 01062
editor@perugiapress.com
perugiapress.com

*In memory of Laura Hecox
and with affection for Pop*

CONTENTS

TWO

ADMISSION

You're older the minute you're in,
behind you the machined mirror of sea.

Here is your self in the darkness—
dendrites, veins, nodes,

eyes creaked at the hinges,
egress of light from the lens,

the acrylic case of your heart,
numbers and curated notes.

The idea here is *remember.*
This is the exhibit *belonging.*

Outside these objects would blind you
if held in the swirl of sun.

ONE

PATOIS

When she spoke, birds came out her mouth,
every word a different species. Thus the civic sorrow
of mass extinction became for her a personal affront—
her vocabulary contracted by 200 feathered words a day.

Her dictionary: *A Guide to Birds*—glossy plates, antique precision,
aquatints of wings and eyes—all of it so out of date. By then we typed.
In the end, she uttered a few remaining jays and doves.
She stuttered strings of starlings, cawed a garbage bird or two—

then grew quiet as a tree, sighed a final pair of finches.
She died, her mouth ajar and nestless. We texted our regrets.
We pen-scratched bits on paper and threw them toward her grave.
The air was empty, the grass and branches cheerless ash.

We felt sorry then. We wanted at least a flock of chimney swifts
to empty out her skull, rise mute and furious toward the moon.

IDENTIFICATION

I wonder why I even went back to school. Like, I have to memorize the names of 100 native plants by December. Like, I have to remember what they look like. Like, I know it's not supposed to be easy, but still.

—Barista at Coffeetopia

Outside the door of the coffee shop
the barista balls her apron up,
unlocks her bike. Around her, specimens queue
by common name—Alum Root, Apache Plum.
One by one down to the smoke shop
an alphabet of plants: Bad Dog, Balloon Flower.
She mouths the names she knows, jostles
with acknowledgment: *dicot, monocot.*

All of it like. Like when she drove out here
in her boyfriend's car and looking
at all the western vistas and scrubby wild,
she thought, *I want to know all this.*
But how this knowing grew in her—a savage plant,
stem and leaves obscuring what joy
she had before: the simple sun, the nameless clouds.

She's grown blind with sight!
Oh, to let it go, syllable by syllable
each name picking up and off.
Let the wind. Let the light. Let her sweater
lift from her shoulders like—petals
of a Flannel Bush, a Gambleweed, a Fiddleneck.

THE SELF MUSEUM

How sad to be alone.

Shoulder door, sternum door,
a single docent heart
at her waxy desk of ribs.

Brass knob and bells, the double doors.
Mind the step. Step the mind—the great escape
is right inside.
Here's the glossy guide.
Here's a map with notes and arrows.

What gentle forgetting life is.
Outside, the day curls in on itself, clouded up with cars.

Inside, I spend my days writing notes on cards:
self-censored, self-deceptive,
selfsame, self-made, self-talk, self-ish.

On display from the permanent collection:
pinch-bowls
pop-up cards
kinder painting—a dog with braces,
an astronaut in a field of multicolored stars.

In this room, contemporary issues: perhaps
there is no self.
I think
the me in me
is gone.

Downstairs: early influences—
a trip I took of seeing stuff,
other towns, other seas, other me's,
a world of humans and their breath.

Did you know? Some human languages can't be written,
  self museums smushed together on the bus,
      bell lines pulled with shelves and shelves of hands.

(Oh brothers and sisters,
sometimes our shoulders touch
and how your touch instructs!)

    Ourselves on benches in the rain.
          Ourselves restless in our seats.
              Ourselves assembled in shared graves.

That's what I mean by gone.
Absence. The concept
of emptiness. How sad
          to be alone.

I will share some details:
    what I had for dinner
    what I did last night
    my thoughts on governance.

I will not exhibit a blown-up photo
of my erection
because I am not a man.
    This is not a place where up is out.

See what I mean? The outside
in this instance is not related to the in.

All my junk is hid,
      uncataloged, boxed, locked, unlit.
      (Though member events are held there on occasion.
      Please inquire at the desk.)

                    Sky of cloud cornets, yellow sticky
notes
                of stars come out—
        self-doubt, self-distance.
                    I forget exactly who I am.

My docent heart
weeps into her vena cava hands.
I'm a private person.

The museum is closed right now.
Come back.

        Come back!
        I mean it. I miss you, Baby.
I miss the way you touch me, the way you say
you understand.

            I would open up for you:
my arms, my door, my legs, the jealousies of my eyes,
all my secret stuff I would show you when
it's night like this and I can't see myself

and I believe

   I'm gone.

Baby, visit the touch tank of me,
the mollusk parts. Gently put your hands in there—

I would bare myself for you and what is bare?
  Skin? Bones? Absence? Fur coat? Black box.

     You are a museum too.
And you and you. I close my eyes and so:

animals, ore, leaf, sky.
How sad to be a bone.
What a gorgeous mess we are.

  Labels on our walls, guides rolled
  in our palms like billy clubs.
      We patrol the halls of us at night.

      We alarm the double doors.
   Museum lights blink off.
Oh Baby, visit me. Visit me.

THE BEGINNER'S GUIDE TO BIRDING

Western King Bird. Could also be
Ash-Throated Flycatcher. I search
window sashes, roof hips.

I was blind before. I was alone.
Splayed around me, guidebooks illustrate

what I think I saw. Eye rings,
throat patch, scissor tail.

Jesus bugs break the surface.
Flocks rise in purple swaths.

I search branches and meadow grasses—
flutter stories, glimmer shame.

Sorrow oh sorrow, stop
calling my name. Courage,
come nest in my eaves.

Perching birds, Nightjars, Swifts.
I was blind before. I was alone.

MICROGRAPHIA

with excerpts from Robert Hooke's 1665 book

What is looking made of?
The naturalist saw in the planet of his eye,
drew with his quaking imperfect hand,

wanted with his furious, damaged will. He wrote:
the imperfections of our senses
and listed figures with letters and numbers,

annotated: proleg, mesoleg—
a biting body enlarged and unfolded from his book.
He titled it: *observations and inquiries.*

What startles so? Pen in his hand,
glass lens, a tube filigreed in angels.
Look: minute bodies, little stars of snow,

a human cell like a honeyed room,
monkish writing on the walls—
manuscripts of illuminated ribosomes.

RAVEN

The raven lived behind the woodshed,
and for a while the chickens lived there too,
but the raven spooked the hens with his shadow hops,
his devil voice, and they would not lay eggs,

so my dad made them a bigger coop and gave
the raven theirs, and my sister and I
would stand beside the raven coop
and shout: *Hello! Hello!*

The raven would ignore us, standing on his
perch, mean and mute. If we put our hands
in there, he would bite them, and it hurt.
He loved my dad.

The raven learned to speak:
hello and *no* and *never more*
and *the sky is falling.* Mornings, the raven
would call my dad by name.

He fed the bird meat or kibble, and the raven
would make little kitten sounds and crawl
up my dad's shoulder and nibble at his
ear and hair, and my dad would walk around

and everybody loved those days,
there were parties then, my dad
with his leather vest, his artist swagger,
guests who came with wine and bluster,

and the raven on his shoulder cawing: *The sky*

is falling! The sky is falling!
Everyone walked across the meadow
two by two, flowered dresses, lace shirts, glass plates.

My sister and I climbed into the trees—
so many things we didn't know—
and watched from branches, but we knew animals
were all around us in the forest,

and we knew that animals could speak.
We whispered in that tree: *hello, sky, falling,*
and we waited for something dark with wings
to call our names.

TERRARIUM

A painted meadowlark on a painted fallen log,
sketch of canyon and field done in ochre strokes.

The snake inside is still as art, convict-striped,
glass-eyed—and real.

Snake, I also was born in the forest and I also danced
on a done-up stage, hair ribbons pressed over my ears.

Back then each animal had its lair. Now the meadows,
the trees are all painted to give us a feel.

Only a fool holds onto place. To survive, make the place
you are look like home. Snake, this is the song of the kept.

See the crack in the painted sky? Soon the herpetologist
will open the back of your world. He'll reach in and lift you

to twist in the air, coil the length of his arm, your primitive
three-chambered heart will shiver in its three-chambered sac.

This is affection—this tender art they made of you, this use.
The man will study your eyes and skin.

He will measure and weigh. He will note your mood.
Let him study. Let him see.

PEGASUS

Tourists arrived in Cessnas and Pipers,
so we rode down to the airstrip,

knees deep in our horses' sides,
bare-backed, snarled, mud-scraped.

We found the open part in the chain link,
circled the horses at the far end of the runway,

shoving and laughing and pushing.
Together we searched the sky for a speck.

The horses bucked and we pulled at the reins
and they jigged on spit-flecked legs

until the speck in the sky sprouted wings,
a swarm, a daemon, a sprite,

a distant-borne thing, a harbinger, a messenger, and we
ran beside it, ravenous, roaring, hooves, blades, wings,

mud on us, snakes inside us. We chased
a thing from the sky. Almost we caught it.

PARKINSON'S DISEASE, LATE STAGE GHAZAL

Here at night the animals stir from their caves and nests,
all the starlit dens and trees emptied of their curled sorrows.

We made a list before I left, and in the margin you wrote
don't forget. The letters darted up the page like swallows.

Beside your bed, I peeled an orange in one piece and showed you
the spiral skin. What sweet sections—the wholeness, hollow.

I had questions about the world, and you nodded, gave all the strange
things names. Now I search your shelf for a field guide to sorrow.

You told us about bears and foxes, timid birds, honeyed nests
of bees. Now look what the green-black forest swallowed.

ASSISTANT TO THE CURATOR, NOTES
ON THE DONATED COLLECTION

One taxidermy grizzly bear, standing, fair condition.
Albatross skeleton, mounted as in flight.

Domed vignette of song birds in bronze leaves and branches.
Foreleg fossil identified as mastodon.

Eight framed boxes of butterflies, organized
by color, no thought to genus.

Everywhere I look the moon in mirrors:
reflected in the gems of beetle backs,

planets in glass eyes of foxes.
A world unbalanced by so much keeping.

Murder bird. Milky flame of ivory.
Feather thief. Name things. List.

Box of pressed ferns and orchids.
Notebook sketches of hummingbirds and swallows.

Mass of feathers, box of jaws and teeth.
Various bones. Unlabeled shells.

THE CYANOTYPES OF ANNA ATKINS

The color blue
I never saw so clearly
as when gathered in a field
around absence such as this.

The place where algae was
then lifted, an alabaster shadow,
a reversed bruise. So a mark intends
to represent, remind.

This is science she told her father
and wrote annotated notes
in a well-schooled hand, arranged the plates
just so, bound the book with glue,
twine twisted through the holes.

The world is round and beautiful
or the world is flat and dull.
We gather what we see, and what
we feed grows tall—
then peeled back, removes.
That's what I mean by blue.

BOX OF OWLS

Back of the museum, an acrylic box
of taxidermy owls.

It's okay. Some things
are lost, some saved

with salt or drying—
we can learn from this exhibit

what happens when
we hang on with talons.

Remember the summer
we hiked out to the hollow tree?

We didn't know how
we ruined things by looking—

the downy heads of owlets,
the parents' absence disquieting the trees.

Our house had many windows,
so at night we lived observed—

forest in its windswept robes,
animals with flare-green eyes.

Love bears itself. Love waits.
We had babies and made our way.

I didn't understand it then

but I've since learned to explain:

those days were a kind of falling
wide-eyed into glass.

Gone forest, gone windows, gone trees.

I kept what I could in boxes
lined up inside of me on shelves—

glass eyes and brittle feathers
that rattle when I breathe.

WARBLER & NEST

The bird is dead—
stillness perched askew
      paused branch
      in a cloudy plastic box

cup of nest   yellow breast
dust-tinged shoulder
tiny crown of orange
      no song no breeze no dew.

I visited my parents
at their place up in the woods
all the windows facing north like eyes
      fabric across the table
      radio on low.

To keep the bird like this
the taxidermist used
wire   clay   tiny pliers
      arranged the nest
      below.

In the box of me
affection grips and claws.
I say: yellow bird
      fold your resin wing.
      Settle in the dark.

MINERAL DISPLAY

for Lucy Moore, Clear Lake Band of Pomo

Above our bodies, tree trunks, branches,
glinted bits of beryl sky. The ferns and grass
whispered: *Badon-napoti,* water, bone.

How is a mineral different from a rock?
The orderly arrangement of its atoms: lucid
transparency thinned by eons, bound in roots.

May the earth hold enough mercy—
the little girl survived by hiding
in the lake and breathing through a reed.

Where do the dead go? Darkness, trees,
shadows of birds. The lake inhaled.
That girl emerged red as garnet.

ANIMUS

Some people wake up
and cannot remember
their own names. They forget
husbands, children, homes.

Think how foolish we are—who wake up
and remember!
We should spend every day forgetting,
leaving behind what surely will be taken.

In Florida there were once
a people called Malhado
who spoke Capoque and Han.
When one Malhado visited another

the custom was to weep
for one half hour before speaking.
Then the one who was visited
would give the visitor

everything he owned.
Those people are gone now.
Look at us here—our flesh,
our sun-bleached skin, our wants.

I do weep when I see you.
I know you will leave. At night
when we are naked
I am sad and watch the darkness

stretch its chilled wings.

You have a lean and pale body.
Love, the moon is dead too—
but sticks around.

HUMMINGBIRD STUDY

Such stillness framed—carbon tenderness,
caught shimmer, the arrogance of looking.

So too the frail beauty of my luck, children
grown to spindle trees, limbs puzzling the garden path.

Motherhood—I made paper boats
to float across shadow pools.

Once I lived on sugar and sunlight,
blooms in vases, fruit in glass jars,

glisten-shine, a nest with such small eggs in it:
vanity and tenderness

like the difference between a bird
and a painting of a bird, the difference

between the moon and a poem about the moon.
The children stare down from branches.

I will read them a story I wrote.
I will show them this illustration of a wing.

WHOSE BONES ARE THESE?

At the dig box, I think of the oxygen tank,
its lift and buzz, a pump that sighed
like lungs hummed through lips. We want to
last. We want to hang on.

Before the hospital, you spent afternoons
with your feet up reading novels, your long
arms, golden watch, a cigarette, a lipstick case.
Evenings, you walked alone the wide, cold beach.

A kept woman my mother called you, and visiting
I would roll around the velvet benches,
lift up the pieces in your collections—
sand dollar fossils, fishing lures,

wooden decoys, books on birds.
Replicas of mastodon and mammoth bones
buried in a box of sand. We learn to discover
by sweeping with tiny brooms.

THE ANIMAL DICTIONARY

We've named them all and still they slink around.
They fight and fornicate and eat each other raw.

They claw and snarl and mark the world with piss.
Still we pick up beef or salmon and toss it on the grill.

Raccoons assemble at the trash and trill their mottled lips.
Crows gather at our windows to look in.

GRIEF

for Lucy Moore, Clear Lake Band of Pomo

In the wing slick woods
the ravens hop and swoop
in damp-hush trees.

Memory and its house:
the girl who breathes beneath the lake,
what's true for love is true for terror—

men with horses, men with guns,
hearts rust open, bones ablaze,
and each of us decides: stand or run.

Some of us stayed, made a house
with food enough and water.
Thick walls, a painted door

too small for visitors.
Oh eyelash forest. Oh teardrop moon.
Close my eyes and let me see.

SUICIDE FOREST

Lava Caves, Aokigahara, Japan

That year we thought the world was safe,
so to scare ourselves we turned out our lamps.

Rusted dark made each of us an instrument,
every measure smudged with cloudy bars.

So I saw my body glide out a tile hall,
onyx suit, soft leather shoes—

all around us foxes in silver coats,
gilded snakes, glinting feet of newts.

I didn't want to light the lamps again.
Fatal life, I thought, leave me in the dark.

Leave me imagine: cold rock, ropes.
Body: hanging. Body: buried.

In such acid dark, my daughters whispered,
Are you there? Is this safe? All I had was voice.

Daughters, I instructed, *the waltz goes thus:*
step, step, step, and in the sooty glass

I saw us as we lifted chins and knees.
The world is tame and sweet! I howled.

We danced that way, together, the animals, the rocks,
the ropes, imagined dresses and fancied shoes—

until my body returned to me from where she'd been,
through the trees, tin lantern in her hand.

AT THE FRIEND LEVEL

Museum steps, glass door, a volunteer cashier
    who looked up from her book.

Memory is a store in the body,
a permanent collection. Part
of the body.

I became a member, an ember.
    A memory of   you

        curls up to my knees like foam
                all the pale words that describe
                what we do, could do, did do.

                        November, December.

Images shuffle. I watch you walk. You
    walk   aslant.
This neighborhood grew up around us   the museum
inside it   and now on weekends no one can get
a parking place.

    You said: *we live in time.* I know how
you despised it. *If we have time,* I said.
    We don't have that kind
of time, you said.   We did not let it go.
                We kept what we could.

    From the permanent collection:

        jewel-feathered hummingbirds

on silver sticks and acrylic boxes of glass-eyed owls
a coyote dry and dead beside
a row of taxidermy rabbits.

Retrieved: you, perceived: me.

This is what this town collects, this is what this town
has done and made and found, our store
to catalog and exhibit.

I want
to be with you.

We wrote down what we knew
but then let that go. What did we know?
Engender: me, surrender: you.
Stored: you, encoded: me.

Rocks and Minerals Endemic to the Area.
(The way we're stuck, can't move on somehow.)
Predators and Their Prey.
(I thought of you and your hair, how you've grown old.)
Special Exhibit: Dig into the Past!
(Remember when we were.)

All the tools that we can use
and what we found was sand and plaster
replicas of bones.
A burrow underground, a hive of bees,
all the bees alive, a hive of hearts, single bees like amber dust billowing
into the garden.

We are

what we keep. We are

not what we let go.

I read it, and I signed the card.

Stay with me. Join at this level.

Read here where it's written:

members are free.

CENTO: SWALLOWS

I thought I could grow old here
the world was flat—the swallows
up in the winds, beneath a starry roof.

Curves the swallows trace in air.
Below, falling away like the eye of God,
their broken beaks and knuckled hearts.

What could they possibly need to bury in heaven?
Swarming insects near a waterfall
bearing word of the bitten field.

When the blue-backed swallow dips softly toward the green pond
it is a stone tied to a rope hurled round and round.
I'd try on death to find you, gown made of grasses.

TWO

URSA MAJOR

The bears again,
the coats of them, sheened claws—

a crush of bears down by the creek, and me
eating fish and pawing mud and rocks,

damp and growly, and maybe I was a bear
or maybe I was myself,

but anyway I pushed and dug between
the bears' slack skin, their swinging heads.

I thought: I've missed so much of you. Why do we plan
and mend when we have flesh and hair?

Baby, my longing for you swam in me
as if longing were a force

that lifted the bears and me above the trees
so we grunted and pawed the air,

sparks and embers and bellowing bears
keening through the vast odds of space,

and stars slid down my arms—and from
the dark height I could see you

curled like a wisp in our fog of bed,
the yellow light, tiny steps and trees,

and even from that height, even with

my honey-claws, I could not scoop you up—

not your slumber, not our house,
not the wrap of porch, our daughters

in their bunks, not the moths colliding
with the light. Nor could I whisper

with my inky lips and teeth,
my awkward bear-like tongue,

how much I want to keep—
and I know it's imperfect to be so close

but up there in the dark
where bears hunt planet fish, where nebulas

spin and distance shifts with time, it's so beautiful
and so terrifying. Wake up, Baby.

I want to tell you: this is normal. Every night,
a sky with bears made out of stars.

WHAT IT'S LIKE TO SEE SOMETHING RED
IN A FIELD AND KNOW IT'S YOURS

Your hat.
Your husband.
Your husband in your hat.
Or your daughter or your daughter
in your red dress. Or your daughter and your
daughter's friend and one is wearing your hat and
one is wearing your red dress.

By you I mean me.
I mean me telling you what I felt
when I saw the flash of red in the meadow,
how my body processed: object out of place, color of fire,
color of alert, signal. Mayday.

And when I say you
I mean: a crimson remnant in the meadow.
When I say husband or hat I think you know
what I mean, and when I write fear, you understand.

When I stand next to you
at the exhibit and there is a paint-smear of red
on the non-representational canvas, I recognize it
and you recognize it and still we stand there.
We would never talk to one another about it.

We're strangers.
We don't recognize one another, not the other's
clothes, nor context, nor shoes, nor smell.
We will forget each other. We will forget the painting,
the meadow, forget what I tried to explain here about seeing.

When I say we, I mean your hat and your husband,
your daughter and my daughter and their
red dresses. I mean the meadow and sky, minerals,
birds, the planets, the bleary space between it all.
When I say red, I mean you and me both.

INNOCENCE

The cat went missing before bed
so I sleep fretful, listening
for a rustle and cracking.

Coyotes circle and rattle
at the house windows. They whisper
plans, exhale through wet teeth.

I wake and imagine rabbits
in their warrens. I have daughters
and cannot forgive myself for this.

The door of the forest
creaks on its night-hinge.
Whistles, foot-falls.

I walk the moon-cloaked house.
How can I make it last?
How can I save it all?

My daughters wake up
taller than I remember,
all ligaments, keen hunger, eyes.

Warm with sleep, they reach
behind their heads
to tie their hair to tails.

FOAM

A great many universes were created out of nothing.

—Stephen Hawking

In one universe I wear the plum-colored pants. In another
I stick with jeans. In one universe I sit calmly at the sink
washing dishes

and in another I smash all the plates, slam the front door
and never come back to this house again. Each universe
is a globular orb pressed tightly

against other ever-expanding globular orbs, and many orbs
have a you in them and many globs have a me in them, but they are
different you's and different me's

living on different streets with different pets
and better children or worse children or children with heads
of horses or children that are just electronic pulses

studying some alternate kind of algebra
at the hydrogen blur they use in that universe as a table
while the six-dimensional pets hover inaudibly at the door.

The you in some other universe shaves more often and has kept up
his exercise regime. The me in some other universe meditates regularly
and has made a priority of her posture and dental hygiene.

But of course there's a universe where you are obese and an alcoholic.
There's a universe in which you've left me because I have developed
this very boring habit of discussing parallel universes.

There's a universe where I live on strawberries

and cream. There's a universe in which I am a strawberry
and you are a dish of cream.

Here on this planet, we hunch at night over our phones or sit
with cups of detox tea in front of the News Hour, grief and anger
lurching in our chests, the war and injustice rising in tides—

and what can we say? How can we explain?
What tools do we have but our tongues and rustic teeth?
I know it's because I don't understand the math

but it looks to me like this world is all we have.
And how can we have room for more, each universe inflating
like too many dirigibles, each individual corpulent with want?

Then again some nights you and I twist in bed, making of our bodies
a golden cord that connects it all together, and those nights
I look up at all that celestial froth

     and I am delighted at such infinity that glitters
         with the detritus of all we did or didn't do.

VANITAS TABLEAU, FIRST LOVE

Listen, we all want it to last, but here you paint for keeps:
umpteen blooms, heaps and hordes, plums, a peach,

all bruised, slumped, withered up with two figures in the front—
I know that's you and her. Well, it happens. People change.

What you made of it is what matters: a bunch of variegated
tulips, a couple iris, an Amadeus rose, its opera cape of petals,

garland of blight in smudge and dollop—the kid gloves
you must have donned to paint such decomposition.

Love is a hanging man. Art is the gallows at night.
We know. We went to the museum and saw it all.

CONFECTION

for Julie Mehretu

It rained last night. Three black birds walk
in the folds of her sheets: sticks and lines.
What a dream to wake up so close
to an imagined sea. Past the beach, the wharf, blanket of fog,
lines, lines, eraser marks. Imagine wind. What does wind
feel. When wind wakes. *Come close*
she tells her lover, her imagined lover,
her own black legs, long spider legs,
marks, marks. Cut: this is a cityscape. Stretch, this
is what I mean by rain. We're all in it together.
When you wake in the morning you emerge from my body
birthed from the electric storm in the desert
outside the city where I was born. Give me a pencil.
I'll draw you a map.

BETAKEN

Stay I said but already she was gone.
I set the table: feeble sun, napkins rolled
in their beaded rings.

Silver tiffin box. Outside: that tree.
Moss and lichen, damp ferns,
all that tendril crack and spin.

I was left alone. Every dawn retaken.
A paper hymn, each broken note:
gate, road, tires, rocks.

Before she died she said: *too many windows.*
I know she worried about the glass,
the rags and vinegar, the ribbon shades.

Nothing really lasts, she said.
Birds marked up the sky then it all erased,
blue as before. Dark hole, brass horn.

BEAKFISH AMONG TSUNAMI DEBRIS

Two years in the hull of a skiff
this fish, a crab, a worm

together made a sloop-size cosmos,
ruffled in sargassum, sea cabbage, kombu.

Unmoored by seismic shifting
the lot of them drifted east,

escaped this, devoured that—
call it swimming—and defined *world*

as four years and 5000 miles in a battered boat,
a galaxy of salt-stars, bloated wood, a moody sea.

The crab and worm despaired. *Woe!*
they sang and died. The algae—neither fish

nor fowl—just hung around.
And in this dory, the view of blue,

rot, brine, storms sometimes, disaster,
the beakfish swam in jaunty circles, nibbled at the green.

La, he said. *Dee da.* Or: *beware.* Or: *there.*
Or naught. Survival is the mutest joy.

Did he dash about some days? Mad like us
in that lonely bilge? Did he ponder divinity, eternity?

Scooped up now in the aquarium, he has a startled look.

Drawing crowds, he blinks at every human face.

Each come to see a type who lasts.
We press in close. Such black-glass eyes.

Fish, we say, oh little boat, tell us we will be okay.
Tell us our world will last the breach.

Swim out tales of leafy place, of persistent creatures
who stayed the course and made the shore.

BED-MAKERS ARE HAPPIER

—*Psychology Today,* 2012

And so we flip the sheet
float up the down, pull corners
taut and in. You do your side,
I do mine. We fold the lip.

Then we're off.
We don't speak. We *do.*
Cover our nakedness, fetch
our lists and stand and walk
and bend and go and slam.

Then we're back. Take
off our clothes and open
up the sheets. We read and sip
and then we sleep.

                        The night bed
            soaks in human smell and sweat,
            the puff is up in ash-winged urge,
            a duvet crouch of rascal curse
            to nest our hair.

We wake rumpled and untucked,
hook-tinged, barbed,
aphasic, fog-colored, illuminated
and alone, alone.

Until you whisper across the sheets:
hurry, make haste, and then with bells
and trills we leap out

and make it right, the corners
hospital tight.

                        The bed abides,
                phantoms tucked in fetid
                sheets, demon tongues
                in metal springs.
    But we are going, gone.

CRAW

If birds have rocks in there
then what have I

who eat more than seeds
and worms and what's more

have words that grow
and gurgle in the scarlet

den behind my tongue?
Hatchet throat, twinset moat

what winds around my say
and saw, what grinds down

what I take in raw but some
graveled urge for nameless ore

a wristlet gorge, a dry
cascade of gizzard stones.

I asked my dad before he died
how can we keep the words

down and the food in. He hacked
and coughed: *out with it* he said

and that was it. Wings grew
from his back then and talons

curled from his toes and his

nose turned to a shiny beak.

He cawed and thrashed up
from the blanket. He could speak

of course, and said *Feed me!*
Feed me! And because I know

a thing or two of birds, I fed
him rocks and shiny stones

and plastic a's and t's and u's, glinting
shards of glass. He hopped upon my

chest and curled at my neck
and slept that way for days

until I forgot to be afraid
to eat or talk and now I can say

what I need to say and still
keep my dinner down. All those

shiny secret things with eyes
and claws—and I have wings

that flap around my throat
and stones I swallow to feel whole.

VESPIDAE

Paper wasps outside the window
and it's on my list to get them down.

When we were first married, I dug a trench,
propane tank to kitchen and hit a nest of yellow jackets

with my pick axe, and the infuriated wasps
came up from their buried home and bit me on both arms

so when you returned from work, I was swollen red.
You held ice against my wrists and shoulder.

It takes so long to build a life together. The past is pestle-made,
written with gathered water on shattered wood.

Remember the way we imagined living? Balconies
and tiny coffees, terracotta bowls of fruit and flower petals.

In our yard I pile sticks and leaves that I don't haul away
or burn or chip. With time it all grows small.

On the window, pearly dust and insect wings in spider webs,
and I can't help it—I write down: *keep, keep.*

THE TORTOISE SURVIVES THE FIRE

He's at my friend's house now.
In the driveway, we watch him
with our arms crossed, the beer-stained
winter light seeping through fence, vines.

He's the size of a coffee table,
80 years or so they say, dumb-ass slow
but with cinder-burn eyes.
He eats nasturtiums. *We have our health,*
he says to us. *Suffering and the end of suffering,* he says.

He does not say *carpe diem.* He does
not say *bombs away, bottoms up.* Nor does
he say *the good Lord will provide.*
He does not say, *I've been lucky.*
He does not say: *they had it coming.*

The house was burned to rubble, ash,
skeletons of charred beams. The humans survived
because they were out. The bird
(exotic, singing, caged) died. A firefighter
found the tortoise in the ash, walking out the melted

garden gate, all blessed in soot.
He said: *you think that was hot? Let me tell you
about this South American tortoise I knew in '68.*
Not really. There's nothing glib
about survival. Is there.

So either it was a miracle or a thick shell.
The tortoise shakes his head.

Everybody wants wings, he says, but not in a gloating way.
I go home. He's not my problem. From my window
I see my children running in from school, their backpacks
bouncing. It is January. They are young.
I have lots of time.

MOTH EATER

Leave open, window. Flare, porch light.
Devour: gold swift, satin beauty, heath.
Taste: yellow grass, pocked oaks,

meadow ruts, animal holes,
sooty trunks of trees, the crackle of branches.
I am dust-eyed and lair-mouthed.

Plucked flash and white teeth
in sheets of gnashing. I am packed
with leaf and litter. I want what is already gone:

you on my porch step
hushed and certain
in your coat of brown wings.

THE BUZZ

For R, after Antonio Machado

If it were a bee hive in my heart—
      the queen and her attendants,
            transparent wings, dynasty in a jellied cup,

if all my veins were branches,
      orbs of eggs like paper lanterns,
      amber blossoms in my lungs—spinning seed

around my head—when you're close
      I cannot breathe—
          each of us a package made of paper.

When I leave, sometimes I forget
      what we have together. These infestations
          of field and work, the pearly buttons of your jacket.

Outside, the world, its trees and leaves,
      its mud streets and grasses all
          dusted in blousy sugar gold.

Waspy words, wax cells
      what auric hum when I lay down
          and you above me.

MICROBIOME

Scientists become more familiar with the 100 trillion microbes that call us home.

— New York Times, June 18, 2012

This explains the shakes I get:
anabolic, catabolic, my gut-animals
rave for sugar, my snatch-animals
twirl like acid-dancers
in Day-Glo skirts and neon scarves.

There is loneliness in a crowd
like that, damp and mossy,
the clique of single-cells,
cilia, flagella, incandescent membranes,
the sad electric pulse of so many tiny amber hearts.

You say: *I'm hungry, Baby, let's go out,*
so I gloss my lips, put on
my sparkle shoes, slide across the kitchen.
Never mind, you say (so smooth),
let's stay in.

Remember all that medicine,
hooded wardens above my bed,
calipers, chelated silver. I was nothing
and now I'm massing, massive,
foaming over. *Take off your shoes,*

you say, so I sit, geography
and habitat in repose upon the couch.
You cross the grassland and rock walls.
You push the branches back,
snap the twigs of me. Stars appear.

RESOLUTE

I stack the plates, count each one out.
You bring more chairs. Outside, the trees

burst in flames of leaves, the windows darken,
dampening the glass. In this house

we respect the dead. We say: *she kept her word.*
But we know that means her words are gone.

We divide her box of silverware. You take the tiny forks.
I keep the special knives for fish.

It doesn't matter what is missing. We make the best
with what we have. The secret is: carve with intention—

the wish bone floats somewhere in the throat. To calm down,
we breathe in. To live together we make secret plans to leave.

We say out loud: this year will be better than the last!
We tilt our knives, hold napkins to our lips.

GLACIER YOUR BODY

I wake to your body
moon-stretched in arctic sheets.
Snow walk night

and your body is a drift,
cordillera of ribs and knees.
Remember, I went to bed mad?

This scalded world,
engine heat and callowed grief,
stillness melted to brine.

Flinty sky presses
against the flesh of day,
cloud-shrouded beauty

and here: vast chill, a milk
of forgiveness that tosses me
into a silver lake.

Glinty blue in craggy sheets.
Move. I'll be the valley floor.
Listen. Rivers chant inside the ice.

MEMORIA

Ships disappear in it,
cargo too, captains equally,
the tables

where the captains ate,
the cook,
the novel the cook read at night

but not the hero of the novel.
The hero rides his horse still
even as

the pages he is made of
sop up
salt.

My love, I want to know
what happens when you're away.
Where in the sea of me

does you-ness float?
In the darkness of my solitude
your face laps

the edges of my beach,
the foam of you, the fish of you,
dark shapes of you that rise

and blink their spin-globe eyes
then sink again
to some shadow castle,

deep canyons, trenches,
hidden ranges, tectonic depths
where the sea monster

curls his tail
and groans, his stomach cramped
with bones and books.

When you are gone, I invent
what you might be, the far-off shore
where you might stand:

your damp armor,
your soaked horse,
the salt air billowing your cape.

THORN & WYNN

Thorn and Wynn are obsolete letters, now replaced with th and w.

Only a fool mourns loss small as that.
For example my daughters are grown
big enough to heave their own bags.

The old dog died, and the new dog
won't leave fur on the rug.
We took out that hedge. We got all new plates.

Still, I'm sad when I think of those letters:
thin wastrels on the London tube
balancing on the balls of their feet, the ink of their skin,

their stitches and chains, strips
of their shirts, their black-penciled eyes, displaced
between affection and use.

What can I do? They'll be all right.
At their stop they hunch out the doors
and disappear into the dark of the earth.

The world is no place for small things.
Pieces fall down the cracks, bits
get blown by the wind.

Already dinner is over. Already
the children sigh and jangle their keys
when we talk.

BOWERBIRD

Nest of little tricks
broken bits of mirrors

what beauty is
what affection is

blue pins and orange blossoms
crushed teeth and apple stems

the kingdom *Animalia*
we reign over with our flowered crowns.

What you said. What I meant.
Velvet grass covers wounded dirt,

cloud forest collections,
bones pinned and labeled in dark boxes.

Those bower days
the strange birds we saw

darted toward the darkness, blue
ribbons in their yellow beaks.

PARADISE

What an idea we made up.
That it's easy some place.
Some place else. Or right here. We decide: *here*
is paradise. Here on the folding lawn chairs in your backyard,
plastic loops fraying like coronas around our butts
and you made Mai Tais and the sun sets in a hexagon
of inflamed sky, the trumpet vine in bloom,
a hummingbird throbs at the Vegas-lips
of the red sugar feeder. *This is paradise,*
we say and let fly a libretto of sighs.
Mai Tais and the taste of caramel-colored
rot-gut-rum, so hot-sweet
in our mouths—we are mute.
I don't know if God exists, and I think you
don't even ponder the question.
The wind chime, the dry grass, your son's plastic trike.
Paradise. We say the word again and swivel
our ice to the edge of the glass.

MICROFOSSIL EXHIBIT

What's the difference
between this stuff and sand?
Here, the collector said and handed

the curator a battered box of slides:
the Infrakingdom Rhizaria,
the Kingdom Protozoa,

an exhibit of orbs and puffs,
half-moons, gritty lines,
squinty burrs in constellations.

I also shed foolishness,
ghost prints in caves, drafts, lettered
margins, pinched and crumpled bits.

A universe made of marks,
and in the still museum
such small wanting

to be handled, seen, and noted:
frozen luster, what's left of cells.

NOTES AND ACKNOWLEDGMENTS

"Micrographia": The italicized portions are from *Micrographia: or, Some physiological descriptions of minute bodies made by magnifying glasses* by Robert Hooke. London: J. Martyn and J. Allestry, 1665 (first edition).

"The Cyanotypes of Anna Atkins": Anna Atkins (1799–1871) was an amateur botanist and scientific illustrator at a time when women were discouraged from participating professionally in the sciences. In 1844, she self-published *Photographs of British Algae: Cyanotype Impressions*, widely considered to be the first book of collected photography.

"Mineral Display" and "Grief": Lucy Moore, also called Ni'ika, was a six-year-old survivor of the massacre at Bloody Island or *Badonnapoti*, or what is now called Clear Lake in California. About 100 unarmed Pomo women, children, and old men were killed by the United States Calvary in retaliation for the murders of Andrew Kelsey and Charles Stone by a group of enslaved, starved, and abused Pomos.

"Animus": What are now understood to be Karankawa Native American people were called the Malhado ("ill-fated") by the Spanish explorer Álvar Núñez Cabeza de Vaca. He lived among the Karankawan, Tonkawan, and Coahuitecan people for eight years, sometimes as a slave and sometimes as a faith healer. His book *La relación of Álvar Núñez Cabeza de Vaca* describes anthropological details of their lives.

"Cento: Swallows": This poem is made of lines by Deborah Digges, Robert Hass, Roberta Spear, Ruth Stone, and John Keats.

"Foam": The epigraph is from *The Grand Design*, by Stephen Hawking and Leonard Mlodinow. New York: Bantam, 2010.

"Moth Eater": One night after a long and lovely dinner with my friend Frances Hatfield, she told me about a woman from Estancia, New Mexico: "Her family were moth eaters," she said. "They would sit on the porch at night and pluck moths out of the dark and eat them. Evidently, different species of moths have different flavors. Some are spicy. Some are sweet."

I am grateful to the journals that made homes in their pages for the following poems.

Beloit Poetry Journal: "Assistant to the Curator, Notes on the Donated Collection"; "Betaken"

Best New Poets: 50 Poems from Emerging Writers: "Confection"

Broad Street: "Animus"

Cascadia Review: "Bed-Makers Are Happier"; "Terrarium"; "Ursa Major"

Catamaran Literary Review: "The Beginner's Guide to Birding"

Crab Creek Review: "The Tortoise Survives the Fire"

Phren-Z: "Innocence"; "Microfossil Exhibit"

I would like to thank all my teachers: Ellen Bass, Marvin Bell, Kwame Dawes, Dorianne Laux, Thomus Lux, Joseph Millar, Leslie Adrienne Miller, David St. John, my neighbor-teacher-friend David LeCount, and Chase Twichell, who has taught me by example. I am so thankful for Amy MacLennan who read an early draft of this manuscript, and to the Saturday Poets who know exactly who they are. I cannot believe my luck in having Susan Kan as editor for this manuscript, and I am grateful for her generosity, vision, and tenacity. Thank you to Charles Atkinson, Dion Farquhar, Farnaz Fatemi, Tilly Shaw, David Swanger, and Robert Sward, who sit with poems every other Wednesday. Thank you to Esther Kamkar for nourishing me with food and bits of paper, to Susan Cohen for exchanging prompts and encouragement, and to Kierstin Bridger for being my friend and texting me the word "of." Garden beds of gratitude to *mis poetas,* those exhilarating writers, brutal readers, and the best of friends: Farnaz Fatemi (she's the kind of person who gets listed twice), Frances Hatfield, Danusha Laméris, and Ingrid Browning Moody. Thanks to my mom and dad for teaching me by example what a joy it is to make things. Thank you to Rafi for his kindness and confidence. Thank you to Truth Alejandra for telling such good poet jokes, and to Chloe Sky for reading all of it and saying exactly what she thinks.

Thank you to all the natural history museums—in Santa Cruz and in every other town lucky enough to have one.

ABOUT THE AUTHOR

Lisa Allen Ortiz was born and raised in Mendocino County, California. Her poems and translations have appeared in *Narrative, Best New Poets 2013, Beloit Poetry Journal,* and *The Literary Review.* She is the author of two chapbooks: *Turns Out* and *Self Portrait as a Clock.* She lives in Santa Cruz where she teaches creative writing to middle school students.

ABOUT PERUGIA PRESS

Perugia Press publishes one collection of poetry each year, by a woman at the beginning of her publishing career. Our mission is to produce beautiful books that interest long-time readers of poetry and welcome those new to poetry. We also aim to celebrate and promote poetry whenever we can, and to keep the cultural discussion of poetry inclusive.

Also from Perugia Press:
- *Grayling,* Jenifer Browne Lawrence
- *Sweet Husk,* Corrie Williamson
- *Begin Empty-Handed,* Gail Martin
- *The Wishing Tomb,* Amanda Auchter
- *Gloss,* Ida Stewart
- *Each Crumbling House,* Melody S. Gee
- *How to Live on Bread and Music,* Jennifer K. Sweeney
- *Two Minutes of Light,* Nancy K. Pearson
- *Beg No Pardon,* Lynne Thompson
- *Lamb,* Frannie Lindsay
- *The Disappearing Letters,* Carol Edelstein
- *Kettle Bottom,* Diane Gilliam Fisher
- *Seamless,* Linda Tomol Pennisi
- *Red,* Melanie Braverman
- *A Wound On Stone,* Faye George
- *The Work of Hands,* Catherine Anderson
- *Reach,* Janet E. Aalfs
- *Impulse to Fly,* Almitra David
- *Finding the Bear,* Gail Thomas

This book is set in Centaur, a delicate, lyrical, and quirky type family originally designed by graphic designer Bruce Rogers in 1914. The type, first used in a version of Maurice de Guérin's *The Centaur* and named to commemorate the project, was inspired by Nicholas Jenson's 1470 Eusebius's *De praeparatione evangelica*, a watershed book in the history of printing which marks the first use of Roman-style movable type. The italics, by Frederic Warde, are based on the letterforms of sixteenth-century printer and calligrapher Ludovico degli Arrighi.

Titles are set in Gill Sans Nova Book Condensed, one weight of a 2015 redesign and expansion of Eric Gill's classic humanist sans-serif type family by George Ryan.